Harriet Tubman

Terry Barber

ACTIVIST
SERIES

Harriet Tubman is published by
Grass Roots Press, a division of Literacy Services of Canada Ltd.

www.grassrootsbooks.net

ACKNOWLEDGMENTS

We acknowledge the financial support of the Government of Canada through the Canada Book Fund (CBF) for our publishing activities.

Produced with the assistance of the Government of Alberta, Alberta Multimedia Development Fund.

Government

Editor: Dr. Pat Campbell
Image Research: Dr. Pat Campbell
Book design: Lara Minja, Lime Design Inc.

Library and Archives Canada Cataloguing in Publication

Barber, Terry, date
    Harriet Tubman / Terry Barber.

(Activist series)
ISBN 978-1-894593-46-5

    1. Tubman, Harriet, 1820?–1913. 2. Slaves—United States—Biography.
3. African American women—Biography. 4. Readers for new literates.
I. Title. II. Series.

E444.T897B37 2006   973.7'115092   C2006–902303–4

Contents

A Price on Her Head 5

The Life of a Slave 9

Early Years 13

Harriet Gets Married and Runs Away 21

The Underground Railroad 31

Later Years 41

Glossary 47

Talking About the Book 49

Harriet stands in front of a wanted poster.

A Price on Her Head

Harriet Tubman has a price on her head. There is a reward for her capture. White slave owners want her caught—dead or alive. Why does she have a price on her head? She helps slaves escape to freedom.

Harriet dresses as a man.

A Price on Her Head

One day, Harriet hears some men reading her wanted poster. The poster says she cannot read. Harriet grabs a newspaper and pretends to read it. She fools the men and they do not capture her. Sometimes, Harriet fools people by dressing like a man.

This runaway slave shows his scars.

The Life of a Slave

Slaves do not have rights. They cannot get an education. They cannot vote. They cannot own property. Slaves have no **free will**. They must do as they are told. Many slave owners do not treat slaves as humans.

This painting is called "After the Sale."

The Life of a Slave

White people buy and sell slaves. Children can be taken from their parents and sold. A husband can be sold, leaving his wife alone. Slaves have no control over their **fate**.

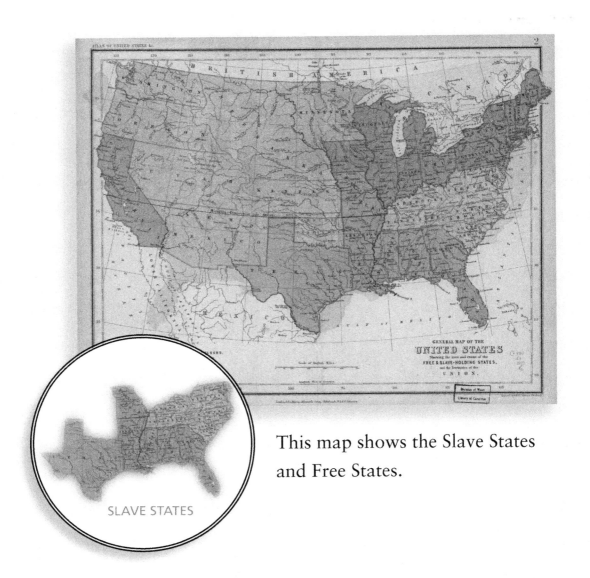

SLAVE STATES

This map shows the Slave States and Free States.

Early Years

Harriet is born into slavery around 1822. She is born in Maryland. It is one of the states that believes in slavery. It is called a **Slave State**. The states in the North **ban** slavery. They are called **Free States**.

Before the civil war, slavery is legal in 15 states.

Slaves live in this home.

Early Years

Harriet's life as a slave is hard.
She eats table scraps. She sleeps on
the floor by the fire to keep warm.
Harriet's master beats her with a whip.

"Slavery is
the next thing
to hell."

— *Harriet Tubman*

Harriet is knocked out.

Early Years

When Harriet is 13 years old, her life changes. She is hit on the head by an iron bar. She is knocked out and almost dies. She begins to have dreams about the land of freedom. In her dream, a voice tells her to escape to the land of freedom.

Harriet cuts wood.

Early Years

After Harriet gets better, she is sent to work on a farm. She cuts wood. She plows the fields. She hauls logs. She can chop half a **cord** of wood in a day. Harriet works hard and grows into a strong young woman.

A group of slaves in 1862.

Harriet Gets Married and Runs Away

In 1844 Harriet marries John Tubman. John is a free black man. But Harriet is still a slave. She keeps working for her white master. Harriet talks to her husband about freedom. He tells Harriet to forget about her dream.

Slaves flee by boat at night.

Harriet Gets Married
and Runs Away

Slaves can flee to the North and become free. Like Harriet, many slaves hear the call to freedom. This call to freedom holds much danger.

This slave tries to escape.

Harriet Gets Married
and Runs Away

If slaves run away, they are hunted down like wild animals. White men with dogs hunt down slaves.

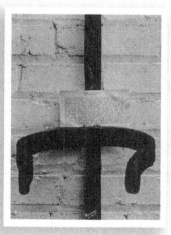

This bell rack is put on a slave's neck.
A bell rings when the slave moves.

These four men are runaway slaves.
White men have shot two of them.

Harriet Gets Married
and Runs Away

When slaves are caught they are
whipped—or worse. Some are
tortured. Some are killed. The white
men want other slaves to be afraid
of running away. The white men
want other slaves to see the results
of running away.

The North Star to freedom.

Harriet Gets Married
and Runs Away

It is 1849. Harriet's master dies.
She learns that she might be sold.
Harriet decides to follow the North
Star to freedom. Her husband will
not go with her. Harriet decides to
go alone. Harriet is about to take a
ride on the **Underground Railroad.**

These white people help runaway slaves.

The Underground Railroad

The Underground Railroad is not a train. There are no railway tracks. The Underground Railroad is a network of white and black people. These people help slaves find their way north, to freedom. These people hide slaves in safe houses on their trip.

The "railroad" is called "underground" because it is secret.

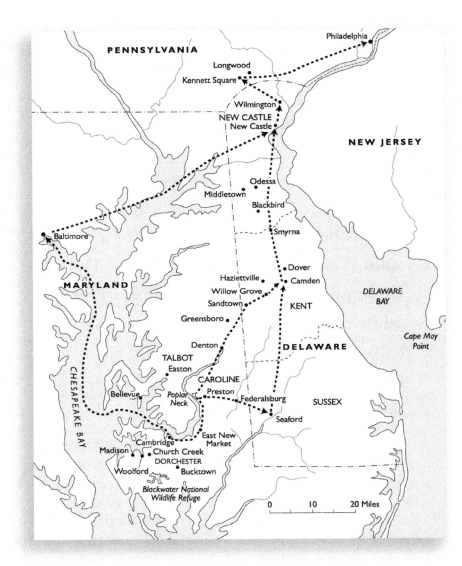

This map shows Harriet's path to freedom.

The Underground Railroad

The Underground Railroad takes
Harriet from Maryland to Pennsylvania.
Harriet is free. Harriet stands on free
soil. She remembers how "the sun came
like gold through the trees, and over the
fields, and I felt like I was in heaven."

In 1850,
279 runaway
slaves leave
Maryland.

$150 REWARD

RANAWAY from the subscriber, on the night of the 2d instant, a negro man, who calls himself *Henry May*, about 22 years old, 5 feet 6 or 8 inches high, ordinary color, rather chunky built, bushy head, and has it divided mostly on one side, and keeps it very nicely combed; has been raised in the house, and is a first rate dining-room servant, and was in a tavern in Louisville for 18 months. I expect he is now in Louisville trying to make his escape to a free state, (in all probability to Cincinnati, Ohio.) Perhaps he may try to get employment on a steamboat. He is a good cook, and is handy in any capacity as a house servant. Had on when he left, a dark cassinett coatee, and dark striped cassinett pantaloons, new—he had other clothing. I will give $50 reward if taken in Louisvill; 100 dollars if taken one hundred miles from Louisville in this State, and 150 dollars if taken out of this State, and delivered to me, or secured in any jail so that I can get him again.   WILLIAM BURKE.

Bardstown, Ky., September 3d, 1838.

Runaway slave ad

34

The Underground Railroad

Now, Harriet can live a life free of danger. She chooses not to. Harriet wants other slaves to taste freedom. Harriet wants to help other slaves escape to the North. Harriet must return to the South to help them escape.

Harriet helps to free slaves.

The Underground Railroad

Harriet makes 13 trips to the South. She helps to free about 70 slaves between 1850 and 1860. Harriet helps to free her parents and four brothers. She also helps to free friends. Harriet risks her life to help others. Harriet is so brave.

Harriet Tubman

The Underground Railroad

Harriet becomes known as the "Moses of her people." Just like Moses in the Bible, Harriet helps lead her people to a better life. Harriet is proud of her work on the Underground Railroad. She says: "I never ran my train off the track and I never lost a passenger."

HARRIET TUBMAN.

Harriet Tubman during the Civil War.

Later Years

Harriet never stops helping others. She fights in the Civil War. In one **raid,** she helps free over 700 slaves. After the war, Harriet fights for black rights. She also fights for women's right to vote.

The Civil War goes from 1861 to 1865. The North wins the war.

These people live in Harriet's home. Harriet is on the left.

Later Years

In 1896, Harriet buys 25 acres of land. She opens a home for black people who are poor and sick. She cares for these people.

Harriet Tubman in 1912.

Later Years

On March 10, 1913, Harriet Tubman dies. She is 91 years old. Harriet Tubman lived her life to help other people. She risked her life many times. She won freedom for many people.

Glossary

ban: an official order that forbids something.

cord: a pile of wood that is 4 feet wide, 4 feet high, and 8 feet long.

fate: what finally happens to someone or something.

free state: a state that does not allow slavery.

free will: able to make choices.

raid: a sudden attack.

slave state: a state that allows slavery.

Underground Railroad: a network of people that helps escaped slaves find their way to freedom.

Talking About the Book

What did you learn about Harriet Tubman?

What did you learn about the
Underground Railroad?

What does freedom mean to you?

Why do you think it used to be illegal
to teach a slave to read?

How did Harriet Tubman make the lives
of others better?

Picture Credits

CPSIA information can be obtained at www.ICGtesting.com
Printed in the USA
BVOW09s0226310816

460711BV00010B/54/P

9 781894 59346